APOLOGETICS FOR TEENS

The Problem of Evil

Apologetics for Teens
The Problem of Evil

Bethany Kaldas

ST SHENOUDA PRESS
SYDNEY, AUSTRALIA
2022

Apologetics for Teens: The Problem of Evil
Bethany Kaldas

COPYRIGHT © 2022
St. Shenouda Press

All rights reserved. Except for brief quotations in critical publications or reviews, no part of this book may be reproduced in any manner without prior written permission from the publisher.

ST SHENOUDA PRESS
8419 Putty Rd,
Putty, NSW, 2330
Sydney, Australia

www.stshenoudapress.com

ISBN 13: 978-0-6455543-1-1

All scripture quotations, unless otherwise indicated, are taken from the New King James Version®. Copyright © 1982 by Thomas Nelson, Inc. Used by permission. All rights reserved.

Contents

Introduction   9

The Logical Problem of Evil   15
The Probalistic Problem of Evil   29
The Existential Emotional Problem of Evil   35
The Great Solution   43

Conclusion   53

Appendix 1: Quotes Not to be Missed   55
Appendix 2: Job the Righteous   59
Appendix 3: Mary the Mother of God   62
References   65

Acknowledgement

I cannot thank my family enough for all their patience and assistance putting this together. Special thanks to Fr Antonios, whose 'The Problem of Evil' talk was the foundational source of the information and structure in this book, and who lent me and endless supply of research material.

Also, a big thanks goes to the Alethia apologetics team who have established a number of meetings around this subject area (among others) and allowed for open discussion about our faith.

God bless you all and may the love of Christ fill every aspect of your life, through hard times and good.

INTRODUCTION

The Problem of Evil

> 'Since times are not hidden from the Almighty,
> Why do those who know Him see not His days?...
> Some snatch the fatherless from the breast,
> And take a pledge from the poor.
> They cause the poor to go naked, without clothing;
> And they take away the sheaves from the hungry.
> They press out oil within their walls,
> And tread winepresses, yet suffer thirst.
> The dying groan in the city,
> And the souls of the wounded cry out;
> Yet God does not charge them with wrong.'
>
> (Job 24:1, 9-12, NKJV)

The world is not always a nice place. If you take a moment to think about all the bad things in the world, I bet you'd start to think the list was endless. Nature itself seems against us when communities are assaulted by floods, fires, diseases, raging storms and countless other disasters over which we have no control, senseless and brutal forces that take lives without discrimination—and that's before we even begin to think about all the human destruction in the world.

No matter who you are, I have no doubt in my mind that you have suffered in this world—a suffering you could not prevent, whether it be illness or bullying or the loss of a loved one or even just a pervading feeling of loneliness or depression. And I'm sure that everyone you know has gone through the same thing, in some shape or form. Despite all the differences in all the people in the world, we all seem to have that in common—we are all suffering, we are all afflicted by the world we are in. Whether we like to think about it or not, and no matter how optimistic we are, we cannot deny that there is a lot of evil in the world.

None of this should be a surprise to you, but if you're a Christian reading this—does this cause a problem for your faith?

Think about it—what do we know about God? What have we always been taught about Him?

> 'And we have known and believed the love that God has for us. God is love, and he who abides in love abides in God, and God in him.'
> (1 John 4:16)

It's the answer to every Sunday School question: 'God is love'. In Christianity, we have the firm belief that God is three things:

- » All-good/loving
- » All-powerful
- » All-knowing

Can you see the problem yet? If God is omnipotent (all-powerful)—He can do whatever He wants—and He is all-loving... then why doesn't He stop the evil in the world? Why did He create a world in which there could be evil in the first place?

Plenty of people have asked this question: If God is all-good and all-powerful, then why is there evil in the world?

For many of these people, the answer is simple: God does not exist. It is one way of making sense of the darkness in the world around us—there simply is no good, powerful God

> 'Is he [God] willing to prevent evil, but not able?
> then is he impotent.
> Is he able, but not willing?
> then is he malevolent.
> Is he both able and willing?
> whence then is evil?'
>
> (DAVID HUME, DIALOGUES CONCERNING NATURAL RELIGION)

What is Apologetics?

'Reasoned arguments or writings in justification of something, typically a theory or religious doctrine.'
(Lexico.com)

Throughout your life, you're bound to run into people who confront your faith, who have different beliefs and question yours. You can, of course, let it slide and avoid the question. This is often a wise decision—but sometimes, it is actually worth addressing the issues non-believers raise with rational arguments. Not only does it show that Christianity is not a 'blind' religion of people who don't use their brains, but it can also strengthen your own faith and maybe even change someone else's perception of God or religion.

But remember, apologetics is a defence, not an attack! We are trying to reason, to create a sense of understanding, not hostile argument for the sake of proving someone wrong. Our goal, as Christians, is not to be right but to follow the Truth, because Christ is the Truth.

'But sanctify the Lord God in your hearts, and always be ready to give a defence to everyone who asks you a reason for the hope that is in you, with meekness and fear.'
(1 Peter 3:15)

who could stop it. But that seems too quick an answer—is there really no way for the Christian God and a world with evil to co-exist? Is there no way to reconcile these two parts of our life—perhaps the biggest parts of any Christian's life—to reasonably and logically believe in the God of love while still acknowledging that the world is full of pain and wrongdoing?

It is not a question we can ignore. Throughout your life—if it hasn't happened already—people are going to question the existence of God based on the fact that there is so much evil in the world. It's a reasonable question to ask—and for many Christians, it is important to understand an answer to it in order to be able to live an authentic Christian faith.

Lucky for us, this discussion has been going on for way longer than any of us have been alive. It's even got a name: the Problem of Evil. And through these many centuries of debate and discussion, both Christians and secular philosophers alike have found that to simply say that God does not exist is not a sufficient answer. There's more to the story here. In fact, there are at least three stories here, because even the problem is not as simple as we first thought.

The Problem of Evil can be broken down into three varieties:

1. **The Logical Problem of Evil:** Is it logically possible that an all-good, all-powerful God can exist in a world with evil in it?

2. **The Probabilistic Problem of Evil:** Even if it is logically possible, how could a good God allow so much evil in the world?

3. **The Emotional/Existential Problem of Evil:** How could an all-good, all-powerful God treat me or other people like this?

In this book, we're going to talk about how the Christian can answer these question—because we do have answers to these questions, and none of our answers involve God not existing.

> Even some of our greatest saints and forefathers have asked why God allows evil to happen!
>
> 'My God, My God, why have You forsaken Me? Why are You so far from helping Me, And from the words of My groaning?'
> (Psalm 22:1)

But before we dive into all these problems of evil, it's worth mentioning that asking these questions is natural, especially if you've been hurt or experienced deep loss in your life, or if you've had to watch someone else go through something hard. Pain and suffering are things that we're never going to be able to get rid of in our lives on Earth, and even the greatest saints have questioned why God allows such evil to happen. But it's also worth considering that even knowing the logical answers to these questions probably won't take the pain away—knowing why you're suffering doesn't always make the hurt any less. Answers are one thing, but healing comes from somewhere else, and we'll talk about that closer to the end of this journey.

For now, let's begin by diving into the Logical Problem of Evil!

1

THE
LOGICAL
PROBLEM OF EVIL?

> 'GREAT is our Lord, and MIGHTY in power;
> His UNDERSTANDING is INFINITE.'
> (Psalm 147:5, NKJV)

BIG QUESTION: Is it logically possible that an all-good, all-powerful God can exist in a world with evil in it?

When considering the Problem of Evil, this version of the dilemma is probably what most people immediately think of. It seems to make very little sense that a God who could do whatever He wanted and is the ultimate source of all love and goodness would just allow evil in the world He made. If He's all-powerful, He should be able to stop it. If He's all-good, He should want to stop it. And if He's both, He should do what He wants and actually stop the evil in the world—right?

Before we go on to look at how a Christian can answer such a question, it's important that we establish exactly what we mean when we say 'evil'.

What is Evil?

> 'What is evil? The question, however, is badly phrased, for it implies that evil is "something." ... For the Fathers, indeed, evil is an insufficiency, a vice, an imperfection, not a nature, but what is lacking in nature in order for it to be perfect ... they think that evil does not exist, that it is only a deprivation of being.'
> (Lossky, Vladimir. 2017, pp. 95-96.)

When faced with the something terrible—hatred, murder, disaster, death, grief—it's really tempting to think of evil as being a force of power in the world.

Even in popular media, how is evil represented? In villains and monsters—TV shows and storybooks not only give evil a form, they give it a face and often a name, sometimes even a personality. These sorts of images are helpful in one way—they help us to understand how these evils in the world work and how we can fight them. A good example is someone like Voldemort in J. K. Rowling's fantasy series, *Harry Potter*: He's the main villain of the series, he has a backstory and a personality and everything, but for our purposes, we can see him as the personification of violence and selfishness. And what was Voldemort's biggest motivator? Fear of death—he was terrified of dying, and that was what prompted him to commit such horrible acts in the story. By giving evil a face and form, we can learn that violence and selfishness is often motivated by fear, and that to combat such evils, we ourselves cannot share in this fear of death, but must be ready to face it courageously. Obviously, there's more to Voldemort's character than personifying the fear of death, but you get the point. It's a great series, if you haven't read it—go do that now.

But although there are benefits to thinking of evil as a thing in and of itself—is that what evil is really like in the world?

From a Christian point of view, evil and good are not two sides of the same coin—they are not equal and opposite forces fighting against each other. That would make evil equal with God, who is all Goodness. No, for the Christian, evil is not an entity, it is not a thing—it is the distortion of good, or the absence of good.

We can see this when we look at the Biblical word used for sin—the most prominent form of evil for the Christian. The term for sin used in the original Greek of the New Testament is *'hamartia'*, which means 'to miss the mark'. It's like, if you're in archery class and you're trying to shoot the arrow at the target and you miss, you have committed hamartia—you have missed the mark.

But notice, shooting the arrow and hitting the target is a good thing. Shooting the arrow and missing the target is exactly the same action, but distorted, twisted—and that is the bad thing. But it is not a new, bad thing, it is only the misuse of a good thing. You can apply this to pretty much any evil you can think of. Lust is a distortion of love, hatred is an absence of love, greed is a distortion of appreciation and an absence of selflessness, jealousy is a distortion of admiration and an absence of gratitude, cowardice is an absence of courage, so on, so on...And even when it comes to the greatest evil in our world—death, the final enemy—we cannot say that it is a thing in and of itself. Death is merely the absence of life, it is nothing in its own right.

> **BADNESS** cannot succeed even in being bad in the same way in which goodness is good. Goodness is, so to speak, itself: badness is only spoiled goodness. Evil is a parasite, not an original thing.'
>
> (C. S. Lewis, Mere Christianity)

This becomes especially important to remember when tackling the Problem of Evil, because some will argue that God does not merely allow evil to occur, but that He actively produces evil.

The Logical Problem Of Evil

Believe it or not, some Christians have taken this point of view. Calvinism (considered by many to be a fairly extreme branch of Protestantism) claims that God has complete control over everything that happens in the world. If a child dies of illness, it isn't just that God allowed it to happen, it was because God actively wanted it to happen. If a man murders his family, God was pulling the trigger. If there's a huge tsunami that kills countless civilians, it was God who called the waters forth to drown those people. One of the reasons Calvinists say this is because they've essentially removed human free will from the equation—in their version of the story, humans are totally depraved (that is, we have nothing good in us) and have no control over our destinies, and God has control over everything, including all the evils in the world. On this view, God is more like a chess master playing on both sides, moving the pieces however He likes and sacrificing them pretty much arbitrarily. That doesn't sound like an all-loving God to me. 'For the Son of Man did not come to destroy men's lives but to save them.' (Luke 9:56, NKJV)

> *in a nutshell*
>
> **Wisdom of Solomon 1:13; 2:23, NKJV)**
>
> 'For God did not make death, neither does He have pleasure over the destruction of the living.
>
> ²³For God created man for immortality
> and made him an image
> of His own eternity.'

But this view doesn't fit with the Orthodox worldview at all. For us, humans and God either work together or against each other—freely. And when we find evil in the world, it is not God creating the darkness to consume us, but we who are stepping out of His light and into the shadows.

> 'It is not God who is hostile, but we;
> for God is never hostile.'
> (St. John Chrysostom, Homily XI.5, p. 334, (PG 61.478)

So really, the real source of evil (which, remember, is just a distortion or absence of something good) is not God, but us when we misuse our free will. And that brings us to the biggest response to the Logical Problem of Evil: the Free Will Defence.

The Free Will Defence

> '... it is possible that God has a good reason for creating a world containing evil.'
> (Alvin Plantinga, 2012, p. 423.)

> 'For there is no coercion with God, but a good will [towards us] is present with Him continually.'
> (St Irenaeus, Against Heresies, Book IV, Chapter 37)

So, as we established above, the cause of what we would call evil in the world is not God but human free will. It's actually pretty intuitive when you think of it—what are some of the worst evils in the world? Murder? Hatred? Greed? Genocide? Abuse? War? Destruction of the Earth? All of these things did not need God to instigate them—we humans are perfectly capable of conducting these evils all on our own. Real evil is an active choice against good, and its results can be horrific to say the least.

This changes the question of the Logical Problem of Evil slightly. It is now less about why God allows evil in the world and more about why God made creatures capable of evil in the first place, since that is what has allowed evil in the world. And since God is all-knowing, it's not like He made a mistake—He knew, even before He made us, that we would cause evil in the world.

So why did He make us in the first place? Not even that—why did He make us with free will, since free will seems to be the cause of the problem? Couldn't He have made us without free will? Or couldn't He have made us with free will that wouldn't sin?

Well, the answer to that last question is fairly simple: no, because a will that is not free to go against God is also not free to go with God. There wouldn't be any element of choice involved, and just as evil is a choice, so is love. If you force someone to love you, then is it really love?

Forgive me for using the *Harry Potter* series as an example once more (again, if you haven't at least watched the movies, go do that right now), the parents of the main villain, Voldemort, are a good demonstration of this point. The only reason his parents got married was because his mother was giving his father Love Potions—magical concoctions that artificially give someone feelings of affection towards someone else. She was basically forcing him to love her without him even being aware of it. She had hoped that by forcing him to love her, he would eventually love her genuinely, so after a few years (and after she became pregnant with his son), she stopped giving him the potions. But once the spell wore off and his free will returned, he was disgusted—he abandoned his wife and unborn child, because there had never been any real love there to begin with.

What God wants from us is real, genuine love—love that is chosen freely, without coercion. That is not only the reason that He gave us a will that was capable of rejecting Him, it is the reason we have any free will at all.

This basically sums up the **Free Will Defence**, a response to the Logical Problem of Evil made by an American philosopher and Christian named Alvin Plantinga.

To simplify the argument more, let's think about it in logical steps:

1. Everything God creates is good—including humans.
2. Having free will is better than not having free will (for the reasons already stated).
3. Free will allows for the possibility of evil.
4. Therefore, a world with both free will and evil is more good than a world without both free will and evil.

It's like saying that a life where you leave your house and do things outside of your house, even though you are at much higher risk of getting hurt by leaving your house, is a better life than one where you never leave, even though that life has far less risk. Even though you risk more, and you might get seriously injured if you leave your house, it's still worth it because you gain so much more by leaving your house than you ever could by sitting at home.

So what makes a life with free will better than one without it, even though it allows for evil? St Irenaeus addresses this question in what we call his Soul-Making Theodicy—how he reconciled the existence of God with evil in the world.

The Soul-Making Theodicy goes along similar lines the Free Will Defence, stating that a world in which there is free will is better than one in which there isn't, even though it allows for evil. But Irenaeus goes a little further to say that God created humans imperfect on purpose because being imperfect gives us the opportunity to grow and be perfected as children of God.

> ## Theodicy
>
> 'The vindication of divine providence in view of the existence of evil.' (Lexico.com)
>
> In other words, a theodicy is basically how someone justifies the existence of God, despite the existence of evil.

Think about it: the presence of both evil and free will in the world is the only thing that allows us to grow in virtue, to become good. If there was nothing to be scared of, we could never be courageous. If we never had to wait for anything, we would never be patient. If we could never lose anything, we could never make selfless decisions or sacrifices for others. If people were perfect and did no wrong, we could never forgive them, and we would never know what it was like to be forgiven.

Irenaeus claims that good could come from the evil in the world, and that in the end, good would triumph over evil.

> 'The oftener we are mown down by you,
> the more in number we grow;

The Logical Problem Of Evil

> the blood of Christians
> is the seed of the Church.'
> (Tertullian, Apology, 50.)

> 'Most assuredly, I say to you, unless a grain of wheat falls into the ground and dies, it remains alone; but if it dies, it produces much grain.'
> (John 12:24, NKJV)

We'll talk way more about the good that can come from living in a world where evil exists and humans are free but imperfect later on. But for now, it's worth mentioning that most people who study in this field believe that the Logical Problem of Evil has been solved.

> '... it is reasonable to say that the logical problem [of evil] has been laid to rest.'
> (Michael L Peterson, Professor of Philosophy, Asbury College Kentucky)

> 'In fact, it is now widely accepted that the Logical Problem of Evil has been sufficiently rebutted.'
> (Chad Meister, Professor of Philosophy, Bethel College, Indiana)

in a nutshell

C. S. Lewis — Mere Christianity

'If a thing is free to be good it is also free to be bad. And free will is what has made evil possible. Why, then, did God give them free will? Because free will, though it makes evil possible, is also the only thing that makes possible any love or goodness or joy worth having.'

The Problem of Natural Evil

The Free Will Defence may explain how it is logically possible for an all-good, all-powerful God to coexist with evil that is caused by human free will—but what about other evils?

What about pain, suffering and death caused by nature—microbes, animals, even inanimate objects (which definitely don't have free will!)? Some may argue that the fact that some animals have to kill other animals to survive is also an evil, and that happens regardless of what humans do. This is what some people have called the problem of natural evil.

Before we go on to discuss how to approach this problem, there are two important things we need to establish:

1 Some Natural Evil is Human Evil

Imagine that there's a small town by a river, and one day, the river floods. The floodwaters cause huge amounts of damage to the town, buildings are demolished and lots of people and animals are killed. It's easy for us to look at a situation like this and say that it was a natural evil. After all, there was no human free will controlling where the waters went or which houses they destroyed. But would you say the same thing if you knew that the reason this particular flood occurred was because local construction had so badly damaged the banks of a river that they burst?

Things like this happen in real life all the time. There is a lot of destruction in the world that looks like it was caused by the forces of nature, when really, human activities are indirectly responsible. Climate change is the perfect example of human actions producing evil consequences in nature. Animal attacks are another example—when a dog bites someone, you might think that the damage is a purely natural evil, but if you knew how badly the dog had been treated by its owner, would you think the same thing? The same goes for animals that are forced out of their natural habitats by human activities, or diseases that come about through humans doing strange things with other organisms.

In short, there are a lot of evils out there that looks like natural evils, but have really been indirectly caused by the abuse of human free will.

2 Nothing in Nature is Evil

We've already touched on this before, but it's worth saying again: nothing God has made is inherently evil. That includes the microbes that cause diseases, the spiders that have deadly bites, the fires that burn down houses—these things can all cause immense amounts of pain and death, but it is the pain and death that are evil, not the things that cause them.

If a rock falls on someone's head accidentally and kills them, their death was an evil thing, and the suffering of their loved ones is also evil. But the rock is not evil. The rock was created by God, and nothing God makes is evil, remember? The same goes for a dog that attacks a child, or even a virus that causes a horrible disease. The effects of these actions are evil, but all of these creatures are still known and loved by God. They may do things which cause evil, but they are not evil—they don't have free will (at least, certainly not in the same way we do), so none of their actions are moral or immoral.

And yet, there seems to be evil that is not linked to human free will at all. If someone is killed by a bacterial infection, that was not inflicted upon them by any human activity. And yet their death was evil. When we talked about the Free Will Defence, we said that the Christian God can coexist with evil because free will is necessary for love, but also allows evil to happen through its abuse. So why is there evil that doesn't seem to be caused by the abuse of free will at all?

a nutshell

> 'Moreover, by his fall Man also drew the whole of the material creation into rebellion/disobedience along with him, and it is this that explains all the manifold manifestations of natural evil that constitute a threat to humanity, a reality of torment, pain, and death.'
>
> (YANNARAS, 2012, p 47.)

It's worth noting that, whenever we deal with questions like this, we don't have any certain answers, and there are people who will never be satisfied with any answer we give. But that doesn't mean that there is no answer. And in this case, we have some idea of why an all-good, all-powerful God would allow for the existence of evil that is caused by non-human entities.

Perhaps we are wrong about the existence of evil that has no link to human will. Perhaps all the universe is interconnected so closely that when human nature broke in the Fall (a result of the abuse of human free will) we broke the rest of the world too.

> *'For the earnest expectation of the creation eagerly waits for the revealing of the sons of God. 20 For the creation was subjected to futility, not willingly, but because of Him who subjected it in hope; 21 because the creation itself also will be delivered from the bondage of corruption into the glorious liberty of the children of God. 22 For we know that the whole creation groans and labours with birth pangs together until now. 23 Not only that, but we also who have the firstfruits of the Spirit, even we ourselves groan within ourselves, eagerly waiting for the adoption, the redemption of our body. 24 For we were saved in this hope, but hope that is seen is not hope; for why does one still hope for what he sees? 25 But if we hope for what we do not see, we eagerly wait for it with perseverance.'*
> (Romans 8:19-25, NKJV)

Humans have been called the 'crown' of creation [REFERENCE?]. When Adam was placed in the Garden of Eden, he was meant to be its custodian, the one who kept it good and beautiful. You can see this as being the role of all of humanity. What happens to us happens to the rest of nature too. When we disobeyed God by our own free will, and broke human nature in such a way that invited death and pain into our lives, we broke the rest of the natural world in the same way. We live in a broken world where evil has ripped into the very fabric of the universe.

> But there is hope, too. We have a hope that when we are restored in His second coming, so will the rest of the world be, and all the wounds of the universe will be healed.
> 'The wolf also shall dwell with the lamb,
> The leopard shall lie down with the young goat,
> The calf and the young lion and the fatling together;
> And a little child shall lead them.
> [7] The cow and the bear shall graze;
> Their young ones shall lie down together;
> And the lion shall eat straw like the ox.
> [8] The nursing child shall play by the cobra's hole,
> And the weaned child shall put his hand in the viper's den.'
> (Isaiah 11:6, NKJV)

> 'Then He who sat on the throne said, "Behold, I make all things new." And He said to me, "Write, for these words are true and faithful."
> (Revelation 21:5, NKJV)

So to sum up, the problem of natural evil is really just an extension of the Logical Problem of Evil, because human free will and the rest of the natural world are so closely bound up together.

But remember, there's more than one type of the Problem of Evil. The Logical Problem of Evil is probably the biggest one, the one most people think of when they're asking the question, but it only addresses the question of whether there can be an all-good, all-powerful God in the same universe as evil. But at this point, you might be thinking that it's logical for God and evil to exist in the same place—but it feels like there's a lot more evil in the world than there needs to be. Surely God could've made it so that there's less evil in the world, right?

Next, we'll take a look at the next form of the problem: the Probabilistic Problem of Evil.

2
The Probabilistic Problem of Evil

The Problem of Evil

> 'Then the Lord saw that the WICKEDNESS of man was GREAT in the earth, and that every intent of the THOUGHTS of his HEART was only EVIL continually.'
> (Genesis 6:5, NKJV)

BIG QUESTION — Even if it is logically possible, how could a good God allow so much evil in the world?

If you turn on the news, on any given day, really, you're bound to hear some things that make your stomach turn. Natural disasters that kill hundreds of thousands of people without cause or discrimination, violence within homes, against the weak and helpless, the torture of countless animals for the greed of massive organisations... the list goes on.

It's one thing to accept that God can be all-loving and all-powerful and still allow some degree of evil in the world—but surely it's something else entirely for such a God to allow quite so much evil in the world! And not just any evil—evils without reason, evils so horrendous they don't seem like they could be justified by anything. It might seem reasonable for a good, omnipotent God to allow people to die from old age—but why should He allow people to endure truly unbearable diseases on the way to death, or slowly have their minds degrade so that not only they, but also all those who are close to them, feel the pain of their demise? Doesn't the degree of evil on Earth seem excessive? If there really is an all-good, all-powerful God, wouldn't He have allowed less evil than we have here?

It is worth noting that, although we have some pretty good answers to these sorts of questions—enough that we can be confident in the existence of God—we don't have all the answers. Nobody does, and we should be humble enough to admit that.

At some point, I think we all ask these questions. When something tragic happens to you or someone you love, or even to strangers, something that feels incredibly unnecessary and excessive in the pain that it causes, you are bound to wonder how your Father in Heaven could let something like this happen. This is the **Probabilistic Problem of Evil**—how could an all-good, all-powerful God allow quite *so much* evil in the world?

But in asking that, you then have to ask: What is making you say that there is *too much* evil in the world? If you've already accepted that God can allow some evil in the world, then how are you determining how much evil is too much evil?

The philosopher, Gottfried Leibniz, asked exactly these questions, and his answers might give us a better perspective on how to address the Probabilistic Problem of Evil.

The Best Possible World Theodicy

One of my personal favourite theories in philosophy is that of possible worlds. This is relevant to the Problem of Evil, I promise. Let me explain.

Look around you—what do you see? Maybe you're sitting on a chair, holding this book, in a room in a library (assuming you still go to libraries). It's quiet, there aren't too many people around, and let's say you're wearing a red shirt and drinking a cup of coffee.

Now ask yourself—did things have to be this way? Surely, you can imagine a world in which everything is the same as it is now, except instead of a red shirt, you're wearing a blue shirt, or instead of a coffee, you're drinking a hot chocolate. Or perhaps, even more drastic things could be different. You can imagine a world in which libraries are run by super-intelligent owls, so instead of people quietly weaving among the shelves, you have busy birds with huge eyes and keen ears, waiting to tell you off for being too loud. You can see why I like this theory, right?

That's an extreme example, but you get the idea. These are all ways the world could have been, even though it isn't like that in actuality. These worlds are called possible worlds. Some of them are very similar to the way the world actually is, and some are... not.

So what does this have to do with the Probabilistic Problem of Evil?

Well, surely you can imagine a world that has less evil than the one we are in now—let's call this World B. World B is a possible world—which means that the world we're in now (let's call it World A) *could* have been like World B and had less evil than it does now. So why didn't God make World B the actual world, rather than World A, which has more evil in it? That's the Probabilistic Problem of Evil, using the language of possible worlds.

But there are a few problems with this argument.

One minor but still worthwhile consideration is that, although you can imagine World B, a world with less evil than World A, you can also imagine World C, a world with vastly more evil than World A or World B. Compared to World C, World A (our world) is a paradise! So how can you say that World A has too much evil in it, when the people in World C would look at our world and think that if they had as little evil as we had, there would be no Problem of Evil?

A more important consideration, however, is how do you know that the world we're in now is not, in fact, the world with the least possible evil (or, perhaps, the most possible good)? This is the foundation of Leibniz's Best Possible World Theodicy.

If you've ever heard of the Butterfly Effect, none of this should surprise you. The world is an incredibly complex system, so interconnected that we can never be sure exactly how one action will impact everything else. How could you possibly know that removing the 'excessive' evils in the world would make this a better world?

This principle is really easy to demonstrate in ecology, but it can be applied to pretty much everything. Take, for example, the wolves of

The Probabilistic Problem Of Evil 33

Yellowstone National Park (Farquhar, 2020). Wolves are predators—they eat other animals to stay alive, including the livestock of farmers. In the late 1800s and early 1900s, the grey wolves in Yellowstone, among some other predators too, were hunted regularly and their numbers dropped dramatically. That sounds like a good thing at first, right? Less wolves means less danger and fewer livestock are killed. What people didn't realise was that the wolves were part of a much bigger system, and they actually played a really important role in keeping the national park healthy and preventing a much greater evil. You see, the main food source for these wolves were elk (large deer-like animals that eat plants), and once most of the wolves were killed, the elk population exploded—there were way too many elk! They began eating up all the vegetation in the park, and it wasn't long before the whole place was dying. Countless other species of animal that relied on the plants growing in the part began to die off because the elk were eating all the vegetation. It was then decided that wolves would be reintroduced into the Yellowstone National Park to try and restore some sort of balance in the ecosystem.

As you can see, you can't just say that God should remove the great evils in the world in order to make the world better. Sometimes, even though something looks really bad the alternative is actually so much worse! The wolves seemed like the greatest evil in the park, but by getting rid of them, something even worse happened! That's because every living thing in the park is intertwined—they all rely on each other in some way, and keep each other balanced. The whole world is the same—everything is connected in some way, and removing something that seems really bad might actually cause something far worse.

This is why Leibniz argues that the world we are in now is actually the best of all the possible worlds. It might look, at first glance, like there is more evil than necessary in the world, but if God really is all-good and all-powerful, wouldn't it be reasonable to expect that the evils in the world are, in a way, necessary for preventing even greater evils, ones we may not even be able to imagine? If God is all-good and all-powerful, then wouldn't it make sense that this is actually the best way the world could be?

When it comes down to it, there really is no way for us to objectively say how much evil is *too* much evil. Not only do we have no way of knowing or measuring how much evil there is in this world, we have no objective reason to say that one level of evil is ok, while a slightly higher level of evil in the world is not. The *amount* of evil in the world is, therefore, quite irrelevant to the question of whether an all-good, all-powerful God exists. The only relevant question would be whether *any* amount of evil can exist alongside an all-good, all-powerful god—and that's just the Logical Problem of Evil, which we already talked about!

So, really, the Probabilistic Problem of Evil just boils down to the Logical Problem of Evil, which has already been solved (go back and read it again, if you like). Both of these forms of the Problem of Evil are quite similar—they are both logical arguments against the existence of God, which can be refuted by logical arguments for the existence of God.

But when someone is experiencing evil in their own life, or watching it happen to someone else, logical arguments will seem quite useless. No amount of deductive reasoning will sooth the anguish of a broken heart. This brings us to an aspect of the Problem of Evil that is, perhaps, more important for a Christian to know than any other—the Emotional/Existential Problem of Evil.

3

The Emotional Existential Problem of Evil?

'We were promised SUFFERINGS. They were PART OF THE PROGRAM. We were even told, 'BLESSED ARE THEY THAT MOURN,' and I accept it. I've got nothing that I hadn't bargained for. Of course it is different when the thing happens to oneself, not to others, and in REALITY, not imagination.'
(C. S. Lewis, A Grief Observed)

> **BIG QUESTION**: How could an all-good, all-powerful God treat me or other people like this?

I want you to imagine a scenario: Bob, ever since he was a young boy, has dreamt of being a pilot. He loved making model planes as a kid, he studied aerodynamics and engineering as a teen, and honestly he's quite fond of the uniform too. He loves to travel and knows several languages already—the job seems like a perfect fit for him.

But then Bob makes a terrible discovery—he's colour blind. Sometimes people don't find out they're colour blind until later in life, and Bob has just been unlucky enough that his dream job is one he'll never be allowed to do. Intellectually he understands why—it makes sense to him that being colour blind could make him a dangerous pilot. There isn't really a way around it. But that doesn't stop him from feeling hurt—it doesn't stop him from shouting at the optometrist who tested him and storming out of her office. It doesn't stop him from cursing the law that prevents him from fulfilling his dream. Even though Bob knows it makes sense, it feels so unfair and it sits like a bundle of knots in his stomach.

As I've mentioned earlier, the Logical and Probabilistic Problems of Evil can both be rebutted with rational arguments. You can use logic to convince someone who sees these problems that an all-good, all-powerful God is not incompatible with a world that has evil in it. But that won't stop anyone from feeling a certain way about the evil in the world—or about the God who allowed it to exist. This is the Emotional (or Existential) Problem of Evil. It is not a logical or rational problem someone may have with the existence of God—it is an emotional response, and you can't rebut that with deductive reasoning. If you tell Bob he has no logical reason to be so upset, he might mentally agree with you, but he also might give you a whack across the back of your head for being so heartless.

So, how do we address a problem we can't address with logic?

Before we get onto some practical responses to this problem, there are two things that the Christian needs to acknowledge about the Problem of Evil.

1 Evil is evil

> 'Woe to those who call evil good, and good evil;
> Who put darkness for light, and light for darkness;
> Who put bitter for sweet, and sweet for bitter!'
> (Isaiah 5:20, NKJV)

When you see something evil in the world—especially if you see it often—there's a big temptation to accept it as something normal. After all, everyone dies, everyone gets ill, everyone gets hurt by someone else, bad things happen all the time. It's unavoidable, it doesn't seem abnormal, so maybe it's not some strange, horrible thing after all. Maybe this is just the way the world works and maybe there's no point in trying to change things. Maybe evil isn't evil. Maybe evil, in reality, is just normal.

Some people might take it even further—especially when they see an evil happen to someone else—and say that all the darkness in the world is actually good. Not that good can come from evil—but that the evils themselves are good things. A Christian, for instance, might try to tell a man who's just lost his daughter to cancer that he should rejoice because the girl is now in Heaven—it's a good thing that she died! For the record, I don't think that conversation would go very well. Or that everything is relative, subjective, and it just depends on who you ask.

Christians especially should see a problem with this. To accept evil and sin as merely normal—or even pretend that it's somehow a good thing—is to deny God.

> *'What shall we say then? Shall we continue in sin that grace may abound? Certainly not! How shall we who died to sin live any longer in it?'*
> (Romans 6:1-2, NKJV)

God is all-good, remember? And if God created the world, then everything that is genuinely 'natural' and 'normal' (in terms of being as it is supposed to be) is also good. Therefore, anything that is not good is contrary to its true nature.

> *'To be more precise... **death is [contrary to] God**, and if death is natural, if it is the ultimate truth about life and about the world, if it is the highest and immutable law about all of creation, then there is no God, then this whole story about creation, about joy, and about the light of life is a total lie.'*
> (Alexander Schmemann, O Death, Where Is Thy Sting?)

So logically, the Christian cannot accept evil and sin as 'normal' or 'good' or 'natural'. Evil is evil.

But this is not only logically significant, it is also pastorally significant. When trying to respond to the Emotional Problem of Evil, it doesn't help to try and soothe someone's wounds by telling them that the tragedy that befell them is natural, that this is just the way the world is. It does no good to tell someone that they shouldn't be sad, because what happened to them is normal. When something sucks, just say it: this sucks. And it should never have been this way. Not only is this a

Christian teaching, but it also validates the feelings of the person who is suffering. To feel pain or grief in response to the evil in the world—*that is what is normal*.

But that's a bit of a depressing note to finish on. Luckily, that's not the whole story. This brings us to the second point a Christian must always remember when trying to respond to the Emotional Problem of Evil—we have to do something about it.

2 Evil should not be accepted

> *'Therefore, to him who knows to do good and does not do it, to him it is sin.'*
> (James 4:17, NKJV)

Once we have acknowledged that evil is not natural—that evil is something that is against God—we must then acknowledge that we cannot, therefore, simply accept evil when we see it. We have to do everything we can to reverse the evil around us. This applies to the evils we see in the world around us, and the evils in ourselves.

> The only thing necessary for the triumph of evil is for GOOD MEN to do NOTHING.
> (Attributed to Edmund Burke)

> *'Hope has two beautiful daughters; their names are Anger and Courage. Anger at the way things are, and Courage to see that they do not remain as they are.'*
> (Attributed to St Augustine)

The Incarnation of Christ is the perfect example of this—this was the very reason that He came. All throughout His life on Earth, Jesus was healing those who were afflicted, forgiving those who had sinned, drawing people to repentance, even raising them from the dead! His whole life was spent reversing the evils in the world and in us. 'Jesus answered and said to them, "Those who are well have no need of a physician, but those who are sick. I have not come to call the righteous, but sinners, to repentance.' (Luke 5:31-32, NKJV)

> '*The Lord did not come to make a display.* **He came to heal and to teach suffering men.** *For one who wanted to make a display the thing would have been just to appear and dazzle the beholders.* **But for Him Who came to heal and to teach the way was not merely to dwell here, but to put Himself at the disposal of those who needed Him, and to be manifested according as they could bear it,** *not vitiating the value of the Divine appearing by exceeding their capacity to receive it.*'
> (St. Athanasius, On the Incarnation)

Not only did Christ heal by performing miracles, but also by taking on the suffering that unites every human in the world. He was like us in everything but sin (Hebrews 4:15: 'For we do not have a High Priest who cannot sympathize with our weaknesses, but was in all points tempted as we are, yet without sin.'), which meant that He undertook all the sufferings we do now. He got hungry (Mark 11:12, Matthew 4:1-11), He felt physical pains, He felt grief (John 11:35), He suffered persecution unjustly, He was betrayed by those He loved, He even felt abandoned by God at one point. Apart from sinning Himself, Christ knew every evil that afflicts us.

> '*For that which He has not assumed He has not healed.*'
> (Gregory Nazianzen, Epistle CI, 440)

By assuming (that is, taking on) our own sufferings, Christ was able to bring us healing and redemption. He did not make the evils natural—they are still evil—but He made them ineffectual. He took away their sting—He made it possible for good to come from bad, for good to triumph over evil. The ultimate example of this is in His death on the cross.

> '*For the Word, realizing that in no other way would the corruption of human beings be undone except, simply, by dying, yet being immortal and the Son of the Father of the Word was not able to die, for this reason he takes to himself a body capable of death, in order that it, participating in the Word who is above all, might be sufficient for death on behalf of all,*

> *and through the indwelling Word would remain incorruptible, and so corruption might henceforth cease from all by the grace of the resurrection.'*
> (Athanasius of Alexandria, On the Incarnation)

The quote above might be a little hard to understand, so in simple terms, St Athanasius is saying that the only way to for evil—death especially—to truly be reversed was for God Himself to take on a Body that could die… and then to actually die. And because He is Life, by His death—by willing entering into the evil that afflicts every living creature—He defeated death itself.

God certainly did not look at the evil in His world and simply accept it. He did something about it. In fact—He did the ultimate thing about it by dying for our sakes. As Christians, we are called to be the Body of Christ, we are His hands and feet and eyes and lips and ears in the world. When faced with suffering and evil, God gave us the greatest defence. He gave us Himself. He gave us His love. We must be Christ to a broken world.

And this brings us to the true answer to the problem. Christ is the answer. We are the answer. Love is the answer.

4

THE GREAT SOLUTION?

> 'Pain and evil confront us as a surd. Suffering, our own and that of others, is an experience through which we have to live, not a theoretical problem that we can explain away. If there is an explanation, it is on a level deeper than words. Suffering cannot be "justified"; but it can be used, accepted—and, through this acceptance, transfigured. "The paradox of SUFFERING and EVIL", says Nicolas Berdyaev, "is resolved in the experience of COMPASSION and LOVE."'
> (Kallistos Ware, The Orthodox Way)

So, we've already talked about how free will is necessary for real love and virtue, even though it also allows for evil in the world—but this knowledge, generally, doesn't make the experience of suffering any easier. Evil is still evil and it makes life hard—sometimes even seemingly unbearable.

Did God just leave us like helpless sheep, alone in a pasture with no defence against the wolves? Are we bound to be prey to the evil in the world without any way of overcoming it?

Of course not! As God is all-knowing, all-powerful and all-loving, He would never leave His creation subject to evil without some way of dealing with it. He may not remove all the suffering from the world for us, but He has given us a way to overcome it. He hasn't killed the wolves in the pasture, but He has made their bark worse than their bite.

> 'These things I have spoken to you, that in Me you may have peace. In the world you will have tribulation; but be of good cheer, I have overcome the world.'
> (John 16:33, NKJV)

As we've already talked about, it was through His cross that Christ sanctified suffering and death, making them no longer something to be feared but something that we can use to become more loving, more like Him. It is through His cross that Christ showed that love is stronger than death. This is the great solution to the Problem of Evil.

But what does this mean, in reality? It sounds really nice, but in our lives, how do we really apply this?

For now, let's take a look at how this applies, first to our own sufferings and encounters with evil, and then those of others.

Our Sufferings

> 'The Lord is near to those who have a broken heart,
> And saves such as have a contrite spirit.'
> (Psalm 34:18, NKJV)

A good deal of modern culture is dedicated to the eradication of personal suffering. Our healthcare systems are constantly improving so as to make sure we are more physically comfortable, and the media is constantly suggesting ways we can find fulfilment, fill the gaps in our hearts, distract ourselves from the aching in our chest.

And if we're not being shown how to avoid pain, we're being shown how to defeat it. The world often insists that through hard work, grit and determination we can win in any situation, we can solve any problem. All you have to do is work harder, be better, dream bigger.

This kind of attitude might be great in certain circumstances. When you're trying to be a good athlete, or move up in your workplace, or improve in that hobby you just love, that might be all you have to do. But you'd have to be really naïve to think that every problem in life is like this. A chronic illness, the death of a loved one, the breakdown of a relationship, the pain of irreversible rejection or the loss of one's home—these are the sorts of wounds that one cannot heal on their own. Sometimes, no amount of self-actualisation or hard work will get you where you want to be. We all hate to admit it, because it sounds so depressing, but sometimes you'll do everything you can and it still won't be enough. The suffering lingers, the evil remains, and there's nothing you can do about it.

Does this mean that the evil has won? Pain in the body is usually a sign that something is wrong—is our suffering a sign of our defeat?

> 'The victory of his suffering love upon the Cross does not merely set me an example, showing me what I myself may achieve if by my own efforts I imitate him. Much more than this, **his suffering love has a creative effect upon me, transforming my own heart and will, releasing me from bondage, making me whole, rendering it possible for me to love in a way that would lie altogether beyond my powers, had I not first been loved by him.** Because in love he has identified himself with me, his victory is my victory. And so Christ's death upon the Cross is truly, as the Liturgy of St Basil describes it, a "life-creating death".'
> (Kallistos Ware, The Orthodox Way)

in a nutshell

St Augustine (attributed)

'In all trouble you should seek God. You should not set Him over against your troubles, but within them. God can only relieve your troubles if you in your anxiety cling to Him. Trouble should not really be thought of as this thing or that in particular, for our whole life on earth involves trouble; and through the troubles of our earthly pilgrimage we find God.'

It's so counterintuitive—it goes against everything we feel in the moment, but our hardest times, the moments we've hit rock bottom—they don't have to be a defeat. When we are at our weakest, when we are most aware of how broken we are and how little strength we have in ourselves—these are the moments we can really come alive.

It is at these points that we have to admit that all those hopeful slogans that tell us that if we just believe in ourselves, if we just keep going, if we just try a little harder, we'll get there in the end—well, they're wrong. You're not strong enough. You can't do it. Not on your own.

'And He said to me, **"My grace is sufficient for you, for My strength is made perfect in weakness."** Therefore most gladly

*I will rather **boast in my infirmities, that the power of Christ may rest upon me.** Therefore I take pleasure in infirmities, in reproaches, in needs, in persecutions, in distresses, for Christ's sake. **For when I am weak, then I am strong.'***
(2 Corinthians 12:9-10, NKJV)

No, you can't do it. But you were never meant to. Your purpose in life is not to be so strong that no evil can touch you—it is to be so submissive to Him that any evil that touches you only drives you closer to Him. It's time we realised that we will never be strong enough to overcome the evil in the world. But He is. And sometimes it is only when we are broken, when we are forced to our knees, that we finally realise that we were never meant to do this alone.

> **Our glory** is hidden in our pain, if we allow God to bring the gift of **himself** in our experience of it.
>
> (Henri Nouwen, Turn My Mourning Into Dancing)

Our weakness is not our downfall, it is not a tragedy forced upon us. It is an opportunity. Through suffering, we become that grain that falls to the ground and dies, only so that it can spring up into a new and more abundant life (John 12:24). The pain of His children is when they can be most like Him, when we most resemble the suffering God, bleeding out on a lonely cross. And that cross was not defeat—it was the greatest victory of all time.

Your suffering does not need to be a defeat. It is only a defeat if you succumb to despair, if you insist on facing it alone. But when you remember Him, you realise that our weakness is our greatest weapon. When we are weak, when we finally let down our guard and call out for help from the only One who can, that is when He can work in us.

And what is that work that He will do in us? We cannot stop at addressing our own suffering. After all, Christ's death was not for His own sake. We must move beyond ourselves and to the pain of others.

Their Sufferings

> '*Carry people's suffering as Christ carried it, who told them, 'Come to Me, all you who labour and are heavy laden, and I will give you rest.' (Matthew 11:28).*'
> (Pope Shenouda III, Holy Week Contemplations)

For many of us, it is significantly more difficult to watch someone we love—or even someone we don't know—go through suffering than it is to go through our own suffering. Parents, I'm sure, will be the first to say that it is far harder for them to see their child sad or in pain than it is for they themselves to be in that condition. It is this sort of compassion that motivates us to act for the sake of others.

It is at this point that we must finally let go of the question of why there is suffering and evil in the world and focus on the arguably more important question of what we are going to do about it. As Christians, we cannot simply mourn the evil we see. We cannot merely weep at the wounds of those around us if there is anything we can do to heal them.

> '*For Christianity is a fighting religion. It thinks God made the world—that space and time, heat and cold, and all the colours and tastes, and all the animals and vegetables, are things that God 'made up out of His head' as a man makes up a story.* **But it also thinks that a great many things have gone wrong with the world that God made and that God insists, and insists very loudly, on our putting them right again.**'
> (C.S. Lewis, Mere Christianity)

But how can we put anything right again? If the last section has reminded us of anything, it is that we are weak and feeble creatures, incapable of saving ourselves from our own afflictions. How are we supposed to help anyone else out of the darkness if we're in the same night they are?

Remember, we're not strong enough to bear the burdens of this world on our own. He is the one who makes it possible for us to be transformed by our sufferings so they are no longer something we need to fear. Christ saves us in our darkness. So for us to help anyone through theirs, we must be like Him. We must love them as He has loved us.

But let's not kid ourselves. This isn't something that's easy to do. We already have enough troubles in our own lives—how can we spare enough of ourselves to help others? Won't we be putting our own wellbeing at risk? Won't it hurt? And what if they reject us? What if our love isn't good enough and end up worse than we began?

> 'We shall draw nearer to God, not by trying to avoid the sufferings inherent in all loves, but by **accepting them and**

'But if we walk in the light as He is in the light, we have fellowship with one another, and the blood of Jesus Christ His Son cleanses us from all sin.'	'Then Jesus spoke to them again, saying, "I am the light of the world. He who follows Me shall not walk in darkness, but have the light of life."'
(1 John 1:7, NKJV)	(John 8:12, NKJV)

> **offering them to Him; throwing away all defensive armour. If our hearts need to be broken, and if He chooses this as the way in which they should break, so be it.'**
>
> (C. S. Lewis, The Four Loves)

Kintsugi – Broken is Beautiful.

A lovely metaphor for the idea that it is in our brokenness that we find our true beauty, is the Japanese art of kintsugi, where shattered or cracked pottery is repaired with lacquer and gold. The results are stunning.

Caring about anyone else at all puts you

'A friend loves at all times,
And a brother is born for adversity.'
(Proverbs 17:17, NKJV)

'Bear one another's burdens, and so fulfil the law of Christ.'
(Galatians 6:2, NKJV)

at risk of being hurt. In trying to mend the brokenness in the world, your own heart might end up broken. But remember, the pain of His children is not their downfall—sometimes, we must be broken to become truly human.

> 'There is no safe investment. **To love at all is to be vulnerable.** Love anything and your heart will be wrung and possibly broken. If you want to make sure of keeping it intact you must give it to no one, not even an animal. Wrap it carefully round with hobbies and little luxuries; avoid all entanglements. Lock it up safe in the casket or coffin of your selfishness. **But in that casket, safe, dark, motionless, airless, it will change. It will not be broken; it will become unbreakable, impenetrable, irredeemable.** To love is to be vulnerable.'
> (C.S. Lewis, The Four Loves)

We have no hope of addressing the Problem of Evil in any meaningful sense if we are not willing to put ourselves at risk of suffering the very evil we are trying to help others overcome. It's a dangerous move, but it is not a foolish one. Remember, we cannot do this alone. Whenever we reach out to one who is suffering, it is not only our hand but Christ's that reaches with us. And if we put our trust in Him, not only may we help those around us, but we grow closer to Him too.

> 'The leap of faith always means loving without expecting to be loved in return, giving without wanting to receive, inviting without hoping to be invited, holding without asking to be held. And every time I make a little leap, I catch a glimpse of the One who runs out to me and invites me into his joy, the joy in which I can find not only myself, but also my brothers and sisters. Thus the disciplines of trust and gratitude reveal the God who searches for me, burning with desire to take away all my resentments and complaints and to let me sit at his side at the heavenly banquet.'
> (Henri J.M. Nouwen, Return of the Prodigal Son)

It is the unconditional, unwavering, unlimited love of God that makes it possible for us to love one another at all, let alone in the midst of pain and darkness. Just as we cannot save ourselves, we cannot love others without drawing on the love Christ is constantly giving us in abundance. At the end of the day, it was never us who were doing the saving, of ourselves or anyone else—it was always Him.

But it has to be you.

He has chosen you to do His work. Wherever you are, whoever you are with, whatever you are doing, no matter how small. We probably won't solve the problem with some miraculous breakthrough that takes all the pain from the world. The world is saved one small act of kindness at a time. One warm smile, one word of comfort, one gesture of companionship to a lonely soul. We are little loves, small glimpses of the greatest Love of all. That is the real solution to the Problem of Evil.

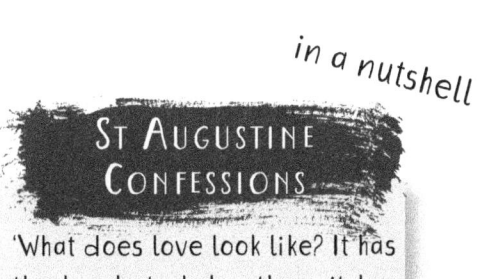

in a nutshell

St Augustine Confessions

'What does love look like? It has the hands to help others, it has feet to hasten to the poor and needy, it has eyes to see misery and want. It has the ears to hear the sighs and sorrows of men. That is what love looks like.'

5

Conclusion?

The Problem of Evil—all those questions of how an all-good, all-powerful, all-knowing God like that of the Christians—is one that is hard to ignore if you live in the real world, especially if you are a Christian yourself.

Whether it is our own suffering or that of others, we all experience some degree of evil in the world. Natural disasters destroy lives and wreck homes, seemingly without purpose, humans hurt each other and the world for selfish gain and we find ourselves in mental or physical distress for reasons beyond our control. It is entirely natural for us to ask how a God who is supposed to love us could let all this apparently meaningless pain go on in the world.

But as we discovered, the question is not quite as simple as it seems. As it turns out, when someone asks about the Problem of Evil, they are probably referring to one of three forms of the problem:

1. **The Logical** Problem of Evil: is an all-good, all-powerful God logically consistent with a world that contains evil?
2. The **Probabilistic** Problem of Evil: even if it is logically possible, why would God allow so much evil in the world?
3. The **Emotional** Problem of Evil: an emotional reaction to the experience or perception of evil in the world.

The first of these—the **Logical Problem of Evil**—is purely a logical question. There is evil in the world. An all-good, all-powerful God should both be able to keep evil out of the world and desire that there be no evil in the world. So how is it possible for the two to exist in the same universe? Does the existence of evil mean that the Christian God cannot be real?

But countless philosophers and theologians have thought about this question, and the general consensus is that this isn't as big as problem as it first seems, and the reason has a lot to do with the idea of free will. We discussed that evil in the world is a by-product of free will, and yet free will is the only thing that allows for virtue and genuine growth. Thus, it is better to have a world with free will because it will allow for

CONCLUSION

real love and virtue, even if it also allows evil, than it is to have a world that has no evil, but also has no free will or love or virtue. When you see it in that way, evil and an all-good, all-powerful God do not seem to be contradictory at all.

However, even after you admit that God and a bit of evil may not be contradictory in the same universe, you might still think that there is way more than a *bit* of evil in the world! When you look around, there seems to be far more pain and grief and death than there needs to be. This brought us to the **Probabilistic Problem of Evil**.

To be able to address this problem, though, you'd need a way of objectively defining how much evil is *too* much evil for a good God to exist. You might be able to imagine a world with less evil in it than the actual world, but you can also imagine countless more worlds with so much more evil in them! And for all we know, this might be the best possible world—we have no idea what the impact would be if, for example, we got rid of all forms of disease in the world. It might actually lead to a world with more evil than the one we have now! In the end, we simply can't say that there is *too* much evil in the world—if God is logically consistent with a world that has any amount of evil in it, then He is logically consistent with a world that has our level of evil in it.

The first two forms of the Problem of Evil we looked at were logical questions that could be addressed with logical solutions. But the third form of the problem is a little more complicated. This is the problem of the actual impact of evil in the world—the feelings of pain, grief, confusion and distress that effect anyone who lives in our world. The **Emotional Problem of Evil** is perhaps the most important problem the Christian needs to address, and it isn't a logical question at all. No amount of reasoning and deduction will give us a solution. It is here that we must ask ourselves not about why there is evil in the world, but about what we are going to do about it.

And if you are going to take anything away from reading this book, let it be this—the foundation of Christian life is that love is stronger than evil. The best and most important instance of this is, of course, the crucifixion of Christ. This was the point at which God Himself took on all the pains and evils of a broken world—even death itself—and transformed them into a way that we can become more alive—a way that we can grow closer to Him. He overcame the deepest darkness of our world so that when we inevitably confront our own shadows, we too can rise in the light of His Resurrection.

Christ has overcome the evil in the world—but that doesn't mean we don't need to do anything. We need to help each other live in His victory, and to do this we must be willing to do as Christ did. We must be willing to lay down our own lives, our own security, our own safety, for the sake of others. We must be willing to be vulnerable if we are to love with the same love that Christ loved us, the same love by which He defeated evil and took away the sting of death. It is His love, and His love alone, that enables us to help each other overcome the evil in the world, and it is through each act of love, however small it looks, that the Problem of Evil is solved.

> 'For while Christ takes the suffering of his creatures up into his own, it is not because he or they had need of suffering, but because he would not abandon his creatures to the grave. And while we know that the victory over evil and death has been won, we know also that it is a victory yet to come, and that creation therefore, as Paul says, groans in expectation of the glory that will one day be revealed. Until then, the world remains a place of struggle between light and darkness, truth and falsehood, life and death; and, in such a world, our portion is charity.'
> (David Bentley Hart, "Tsunami and Theodicy" in First Things)

Appendices

Appendix 1: Quotes Not to be Missed

As you can see, there is a great deal of Christian literature that talks about suffering, love and God—all very relevant to the Problem of Evil. I was sad not to be able to include all the beautiful verses and quotes I found on the subject, simply because I ran out of space. And then I realised—why shouldn't I?

Below is a collection of quotes and verses relating to the Problem of Evil that couldn't be included in the main body of the book. Enjoy!

> 'Both good and evil, when they are full grown, become retrospective...That is what mortals misunderstand. They say of some temporary suffering, 'No future bliss can make up for it,' not knowing that Heaven, once attained, will work backwards and turn even that agony into a glory. And of some sinful pleasure they say 'Let me but have this and I'll take the consequences': little dreaming how damnation will spread back and back into their past and contaminate the pleasure of the sin.'
> (C. S. Lewis, The Great Divorce)

> 'Good and evil both increase at compound interest. That is why the little decisions you and I make every day are of such infinite importance. The smallest good act today is the capture of a strategic point from which, a few months later, you may be able to go on to victories you never dreamed of. An apparently trivial indulgence in lust or anger today is the loss of a ridge or railway line or bridgehead from which the enemy may launch an attack otherwise impossible.'
> (C. S. Lewis, Mere Christianity)

'All the disciples of Christ despise death; they take the offensive against it and, instead of fearing it, by the sign of the cross and by faith in Christ trample on it as on something dead. Before the divine sojourn of the Saviour, even the holiest of men were afraid of death, and mourned the dead as those who perish. But now that the Saviour has raised His body, death is no longer terrible, but all those who believe in Christ tread it underfoot as nothing, and prefer to die rather than to deny their faith in Christ, knowing full well that when they die they do not perish, but live indeed, and become incorruptible through the resurrection.'

(Athanasius of Alexandria, On the Incarnation)

'The body of the Word, then, being a real human body, in spite of its having been uniquely formed from a virgin, was of itself mortal and, like other bodies, liable to death. But the indwelling of the Word loosed it from this natural liability, so that corruption could not touch it. Thus is happened that two opposite marvels took place at once: the death of all was consummated in the Lord's body; yet, because the Word was in it, death and corruption were in the same act utterly abolished.'

(Athanasius of Alexandria, On the Incarnation)

'What, then, was God to do? What else could He possibly do, being God, but renew His Image in mankind, so that through it men might once more come to know Him? And how could this be done save by the coming of the very Image Himself, our Saviour Jesus Christ? Men could not have done it, for they are only made after the Image; nor could angels have done it, for they are not the images of God. The Word of God came in His own Person, because it was He alone, the Image of the Father Who could recreate man made after the Image.'

(Athanasius of Alexandria, On the Incarnation)

APPENDICES

'If tribulation is a necessary element in redemption, we must anticipate that it will never cease till God sees the world to be either redeemed or no further redeemable.'
(C.S. Lewis, The Problem of Pain)

'Christ's suffering and death have, then, an objective value: he has done for us something we should be altogether incapable of doing without him. At the same time, we should not say that Christ has suffered "instead of us", but rather that he has suffered on our behalf. The Son of God suffered "unto death", not that we might exempt from suffering, but that our suffering might be like his. Christ has offered us, now a way round suffering, but a way through it; not substitution, but saving companionship.'
(Kallistos Ware, The Orthodox Way, pg. 82)

'Compassion asks us to go where it hurts, to enter into the places of pain, to share in brokenness, fear, confusion, and anguish. Compassion challenges us to cry out with those in misery, to mourn with those who are lonely, to weep with those in tears. Compassion requires us to be weak with the weak, vulnerable with the vulnerable, and powerless with the powerless. Compassion means full immersion in the condition of being human.'
(Henri Nouwen, You are the Beloved: Daily Meditations for Spiritual Living)

'The sacrifices of God are a broken spirit,
A broken and a contrite heart—
These, O God, You will not despise.'
(Psalm 51:17, NKJV)

'3... that no one should be shaken by these afflictions; for you yourselves know that we are appointed to this. 4 For, in fact, we told you before when we were with you that we would suffer tribulation, just as it happened, and you know.'
(1 Thessalonians 3:4, NKJV)

'So that the one road for which we now need God's leadership most of all is a road God, in His own nature, has never walked. But suppose God became a man... He could surrender His will, suffer and die, because He was a man.'
(C. S. Lewis, Mere Christianity)

'I have received no assurance that anything we can do will eradicate suffering. I think the best results are obtained by people who work quietly away at limited objectives, such as the abolition of the slave trade, or prison reform, or factory acts, or tuberculosis, not by those who think they can achieve universal justice, or health, or peace. I think the art of life consists in tackling each immediate evil as well as we can.'
(C. S. Lewis, C.S. Lewis: essay collection and other short pieces)

Appendix 2: Job the Righteous

'There was a man in the land of Uz, whose name was Job; and that man was blameless and upright, and one who feared God and shunned evil.'
(Job 1:1, NKJV)

When people think of suffering in the Bible, one of the first names that is bound to come up is Job—also known as Job the Righteous. One thing that Job is known for is enduring an enormous amount of pain, loneliness and loss.

Job was a good man and, for the most part, had a good life. He had a wife, many children, lots and lots and lots of livestock (which, back then, meant your were super wealthy). He worshipped God diligently and put a lot of effort into his spirituality. At this point, Job was what we would like to think is what happens to anyone who does their best to be a good Christian. It makes a lot more sense to us to think that if we do good, good things will happen to us, and if we do bad, bad things will happen to us. It's logical, and it seems fair, right?

But Job isn't famous for being wealthy, or even for being good. He's famous for his pain. So, what exactly did he lose?

- » His livestock and servants (killed/stolen by raiders)
- » His house (blown down by a strong wind)
- » His children (crushed when the house fell down)
- » His reputation (everyone thought he had done something evil to deserve this)
- » His health (afflicted with painful boils all over his body)
- » His friends (they accuse him of sinning)

That's a lot! I can't even begin to imagine how it must've felt to have almost everything taken away from you, seemingly without reason. At his peak of suffering, all he had left was his life and his wife, and he was wishing he was dead and his wife was, for a time, really frustrated with him for still worshipping a God who would let all of this happen to them.

But there are a few important things to remember here.

For one thing, although God was allowing all of this tragedy to happen to Job, He wasn't the one making it happen. It wasn't a punishment, it wasn't a test that God was imposing on Job. All of this evil was not God's doing. **God does not create evil.**

Another important thing to note is that the reason Satan is testing Job with all of this suffering is because he thinks that the only reason Job loves and worships God is because God has given him a good life. I think we're tempted to believe something like this. **Do we only love God when things are going well?** When things start going badly, do we blame God for it?

Or on the flip side, when things are going well, do we use that as an indication of God's love for us? **And then, when troubles come, do we then think that God has left us?**

> 'Look, I go forward, but He is not there,
> And backward, but I cannot perceive Him;
> 9 When He works on the left hand, I cannot behold Him;
> When He turns to the right hand, I cannot see Him.
> 10 But He knows the way that I take;
> When He has tested me, I shall come forth as gold.
> 11 My foot has held fast to His steps;
> I have kept His way and not turned aside.
> 12 I have not departed from the commandment of His lips;
> I have treasured the words of His mouth
> More than my necessary food.'
> (Job 23:8-12, NKJV)

Job is confident that, despite how much his so-called friends harass him about it, he has done nothing to deserve what has happened to him—and generally, we agree. He's not called Job the Righteous for nothing.

But as you can tell, this didn't stop him from being miserable, being upset at God and feeling as though he has been abandoned.

But God has something to say in response to all of Job's complaints. In chapters 38 to 41, God challenges Job and tells him about all of the amazing, wondrous and powerful things He has done and has the power to do. Basically, what He's saying is that Job isn't God. Job couldn't possibly know the whole story—he doesn't know why this evil is happening, or what its full impact is on his life or anyone else's, any more than he could control the actions of wild animals. At the end of the day, God is God, and not us. We're not going to have all the answers. Sometimes, we just have to trust Him.

Appendix 3: Mary the Mother of God

> *'Now in the sixth month the angel Gabriel was sent by God to a city of Galilee named Nazareth, to a virgin betrothed to a man whose name was Joseph, of the house of David. The virgin's name was Mary. And having come in, the angel said to her, **"Rejoice, highly favoured one, the Lord is with you; blessed are you among women!"***
>
> (Luke 1:26-28, NKJV)

Saint Mary is known and loved in our Church for being righteous, loving and pure of heart. After all, she was chosen to be the mother of the Incarnate Word of God—there was clearly something special about her!

But, although she is repeatedly called blessed and favoured, Saint Mary's life was far from breezy. Let's think a bit about Saint Mary's life, shall we?

From a young age, she was given away by her parents to serve in the temple. Serving in the temple was not quite the same thing as serving at church in modern times—trust me, if you think cleaning your church is gross, imagine what it's like cleaning up after bloody animal sacrifices on an altar! With no soap or detergent, mind you. Nasty, nasty, nasty. Not to mention being separated from her family. We can only speculate about what Mary's early years were like, but if I was her, I would've felt really of lonely.

When she was a teenager, Mary was told that she was going to bear the Messiah—the hope of her nation—God Himself! That sounds like something to celebrate, right? Mary sung about the glory of God once she had come to terms with her role in Israel's story, and her cousin Elizabeth called her blessed as soon as she saw her. But not everyone would have seen the unusual pregnancy in the same way—even Joseph, her betrothed, struggled with the idea. At such a young age, Mary not only had to grapple with the idea that she was going to give birth to the Son of God, but also likely the judgement and gossip of people who didn't believe that she had conceived by the Holy Spirit and not some random bloke. She would have endured a long period of social isolation while she was pregnant, not to mention having to flee her home and go to Egypt when the king threatened to kill her Baby.

Then there was Jesus. Raising a kid was always going to be a difficult task, but raising the Son of God requires a whole new level of parenting. Remember that time He ran off to teach in a temple when He was, like, twelve, and Mary thought she'd *lost* the Messiah? That was fun.

But the worst was yet to come. Ask any parent and they'll tell you the same thing—their worst fear is losing their child. It's probably one of the most painful experiences a person can go through. Not only did Mary have to watch her beloved Son be slandered, mocked, reviled and unjustly persecuted, but she also had to stand back and let Him be beaten up, scourged, tormented and subjected to one of the most brutal forms of execution humanity has ever invented. I struggle to imagine a mother going through anything worse.

> 'Then Simeon blessed them, and said to Mary His mother, "Behold, this Child is destined for the fall and rising of many in Israel, and for a sign which will be spoken against **(yes, a sword will pierce through your own soul also)**, that the thoughts of many hearts may be revealed."'
> (Luke 2:34-35, NKJV)

Clearly you don't have to be a bad person for bad things to happen to you. Saint Mary is the highest of all our saints, and she probably went through some of the worst emotional distresses a person could. But none of this changes the fact that Saint Mary was blessed, that she was favoured by God, and that God was with her. In fact, I would argue that those are the only reasons she was able to get through her immense suffering.

How easy or pain-free your life is was never an indication of how good you were, or how close you were to God—Saint Mary is the perfect example of this. The world offered her nothing but persecution and pain, but she found peace in the fact that God never left her, even as He was dying on the cross.

References and Further Reading

Athanasius of Alexandria. 1970. St. Athanasius on the Incarnation: The Treatise De Incarnatione Verbi Dei. A. R. Mowbray & Co.

Augustine of Hippo. 1992. Confessions. Clarendon Press; Oxford University Press.

Farquhar, Brodie. 2020. "Wolf Reintroduction Changes Ecosystem in Yellowstone." Outside. Retrieved (https://www.yellowstonepark.com/things-to-do/wildlife/wolf-reintroduction-changes-ecosystem/).

Gregory Nazianzen. 1893. "Select Letters." Pp. 435–482 in Nicene and Post Nicene Fathers. Series II, Volume VII., edited by P. Schaff and H. Wace. T&T Clark; Wm B Eerdmans Publishing Company.

Hart, David Bentley. 2010. "Tsunami and Theodicy: Haiti." First Things, January.

Hume, David. 1998. Dialogues Concerning Natural Religion. 2nd ed. edited by R. H. Popkin. Hackett Publishing Company.

Irenaeus of Lyon. 1885. "Against Heresies." Pp. 309–567 in Ante-Nicene Fathers, Volume I, edited by A. Roberts, J. Donaldson, and A. C. Coxe. T&T Clark; Wm B Eerdmans Publishing Company.

John Chrysostom. 1889. "Homilies on the Epistles of Paul to the Corinthians." in Nicene and Post Nicene Fathers. Series I, Volume XII., edited by P. Schaff and T. W. Chambers. T&T Clark; Wm B Eerdmans Publishing Company.

Lewis, Clive Staples. 1968. A Grief Observed. London: Faber & Faber.

Lewis, Clive Staples. 1977. The Great Divorce. Fontana Religious.

Lewis, Clive Staples. 2000. CS Lewis: Essay Collection and Other Short Pieces. Fount.

Lossky, Vladimir. 2017. Dogmatic Theology: Creation, God's Image in Man, & the Redeeming Work of the Trinity. 2nd ed. St Vladimir's Seminary Press.

Meister, Chad. 2009. Introducing Philosophy of Religion. Routledge.

Menzel, Christopher. 2017. "Possible Worlds" edited by E. N. Zalta. The Stanford Encyclopedia of Philosophy. https://plato.stanford.edu/archives/win2017/entries/possible-worlds/

Nouwen, Henri. 1994. The Return of the Prodigal Son: A Story of

REFERENCES

Homecoming. Image Books.

Nouwen, Henri. 2004. Turn My Mourning into Dancing: Finding Hope in Hard Times. Thomas Nelson.

Nouwen, Henri. 2017. You Are The Beloved: Daily Meditations for Spiritual Living. Hodder Faith.

Peterson, Michael L. 1997. "The Problem of Evil." Pp. 393–401 in A Companion to Philosophy of Religion, edited by P. L. Quinn and C. Taliaferro. Blackwell Publishing Ltd.

Plantinga, Alvin. 2012. "A Free Will Defense." Pp. 422–32 in Christian Apologetics: An Anthology of Primary Sources, edited by K. A. Sweis and C. Meister. Zondervan.

Schmemann, Alexander. 2003. O Death Where Is Thy Sting? St Vladimir's Seminary Press.

Shenouda III, Pope. 2013. Holy Week Contemplations. St. Shenouda Monastery.

Tertullian. 1900. The Apology of Tertullian. Griffith Farran.

Ware, Kallistos. 1995. The Orthodox Way. Revised edition. St Vladimir's Seminary Press.

Yannaras, C. 2012. The Enigma of Evil. (Norman Russell, Trans.). Holy Cross Orthodox Press.

www.ingramcontent.com/pod-product-compliance
Lightning Source LLC
Chambersburg PA
CBHW031214090426
42736CB00009B/918